RAPID PERSPECTIVE

rapid perspective

by **G. E. Wickham,** FRBS, ARCA, Lecturer
responsible for Visual Studies at the College
of Architecture and Advanced Building
Technology, The Polytechnic, Regent Street,
London

NEW YORK / **TRANSATLANTIC ARTS** / 1967

24119

First American Edition:
Transatlantic Arts Inc.
565 Fifth Avenue,
New York, NY 10017

(GB) SBN 85458-050

CONTENTS

1.0/ Introduction

1.1/ Perspective helps train the eye in the appreciation of space and provides a discipline and a guide in free-hand drawing.

1.2/ A quick means of setting up is a must for the designer who needs to confirm what his proposals will look like in 3-dimensions.

1.3/ This book introduces methods of setting up a perspective for a man who needs a practical tool in his daily work.

1.4/ The **parallel perspective** method avoids many of the pitfalls encountered in traditional construction. The **oblique perspective** method is a new development that appeals to those who wish to develop a means of producing accurate perspectives rapidly.

1.5/ However a perspective projection shows at least one plan and two elevations, and often more, and so no one will expect to set up a complicated subject in too short a time.

1.6/ No previous knowledge of perspective is needed before using the methods shown here, but the first pages provide some of the rules and terms necessary for a better understanding of perspective projection, and how they relate to freehand drawing on site.

1.7/ To simplify the explanation in a practical way the procedure is developed step by step. Few contractions of words or initials are used to avoid confusions when referring back to a specific point in the procedure. For ease of following the constructions, the drawings are set across the page with the instructions below them.

1.8/ It is recommended that the double cube grid is first set up in parallel perspective and then in oblique perspective, each point being checked before proceeding to the next. The explanations, if necessary, can wait.

1.9/ The following books may be of interest to those who wish to proceed to a deeper study of the subject : *The Perception of the Visual World* by J. J. Gibson ; (an authoritative study showing the place of perspective in our appreciation of space) ; *The Theory and Practice of Perspective* by W. Abbott (a concise survey of the geometry of perspective and its application to a wide range of problems and subject matter. It includes a chapter on the history of perspective) ; *Perspective Drawing* by H. F. Hollis (a handy-sized publication with a lot of information, especially about measuring in perspective).

2.0/ Perspective projection and spatial perception.

2.1/ If the requirements of perspective projection are met, which are that:

    1) the size is sufficiently large—that is, as large as is practicable;

    2) the Cone of Vision is not exceeded   (see page 24);

    3) the finished perspective is viewed from the correct position, i.e. from the same Viewpoint used when setting up the perspective;

    4) the diminution of size of forms and texture is correctly maintained, i.e. inversely in proportion to the distance from the Observer;

    5) the effect of illumination is consistent, and

    6) a differentiation of tone, acuity (focus) and emphasis is maintained as a progression from near to far—generally this gradient is most effective as from front to rear giving less and less contrast, less detail and emphasis, and getting lighter with distance,

then the resultant drawing will accord convincingly with our perception of form and spacial disposition, and provide a real sense of scale and proportion. This is so, in spite of lack of binocular stereoscopy or of any relative movement of the Observer, both of which contribute to our accurate assessment of three dimensions. (The sense of depth may be enhanced with colour and atmospheric perspective by making the distant colours lighter and cooler, i.e. more blue).

5

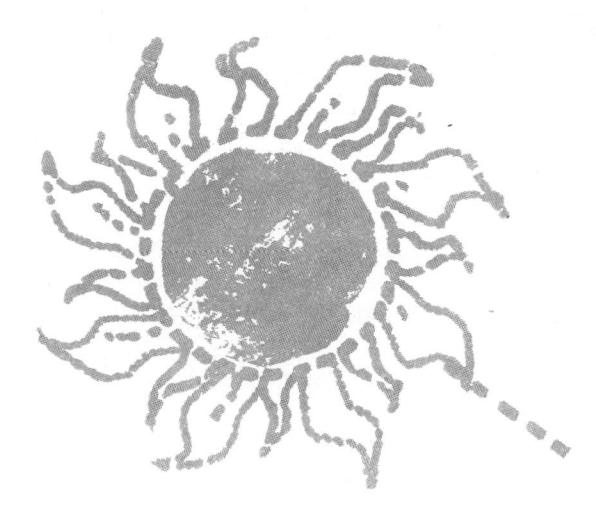

3.0/ Perspective.

3.1/ *Projection to a point.* Vision is the ability to perceive light. As far as vision is concerned, light moves in straight lines, so that each point seen lies on a straight path from the eye. Thus all the lines converge on the eye (itself a point).

6

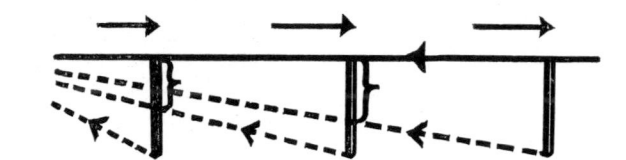

3.2/ *Converging to a point.*   As the lines converge, the greater distance an object is from the eye, the smaller it appears.   Geometrically it is shown that a length as seen from the same angle, is indirectly proportional to the distance from the eye; i.e. at twice the distance it appears half the apparent height; or again, when a post is half as far away it appears two-thirds the height of the nearer post as in the last two posts in the above diagram.   It follows that a length seen at an infinite distance appears to be infinitely small— a point.

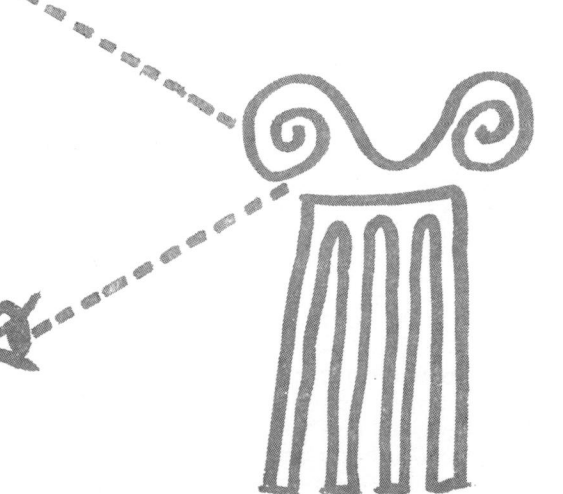

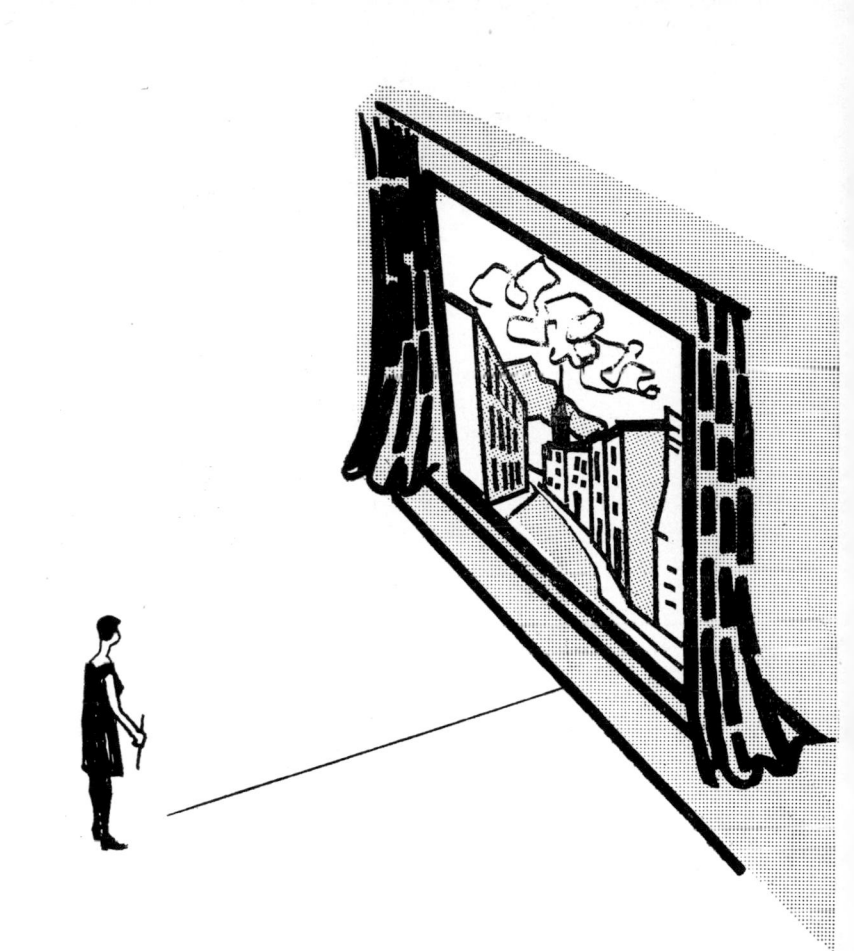

3.3/ The Picture Plane. Perspective is the projection that defines this convergence to a point and resultant shapes produced where the converging lines cut a 2-dimensional Picture Plane (this may be imagined as an image as seen through, and 'traced' upon, a window pane, or, for objects in front, traced against the window).

8

3.4/ Setting up. The purpose of all methods of setting up is to determine where any one point would be on this Picture Plane (in short, how far vertically and horizontally is each point removed from the Centre of Vision *see* 8.4). A line is plotted by joining two points, and areas defined by a number of lines. Curved lines and circles may be constructed (like a graph).

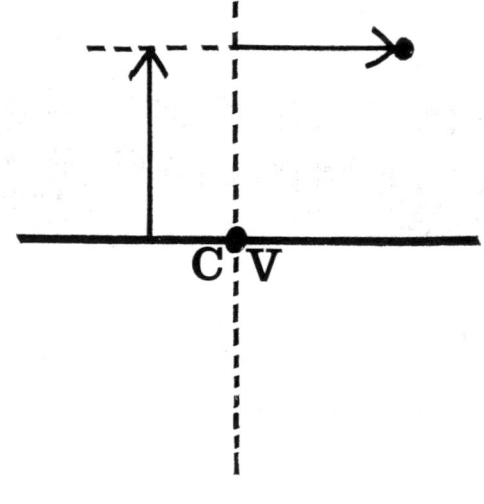

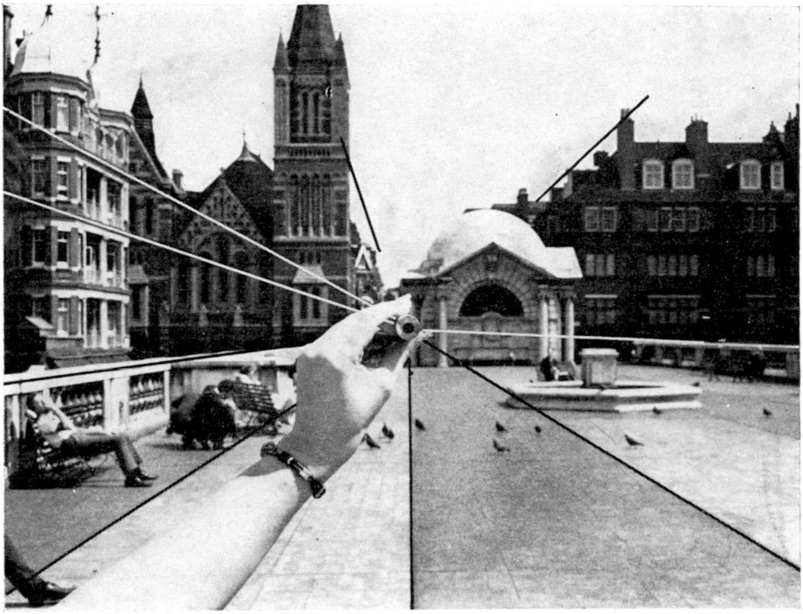

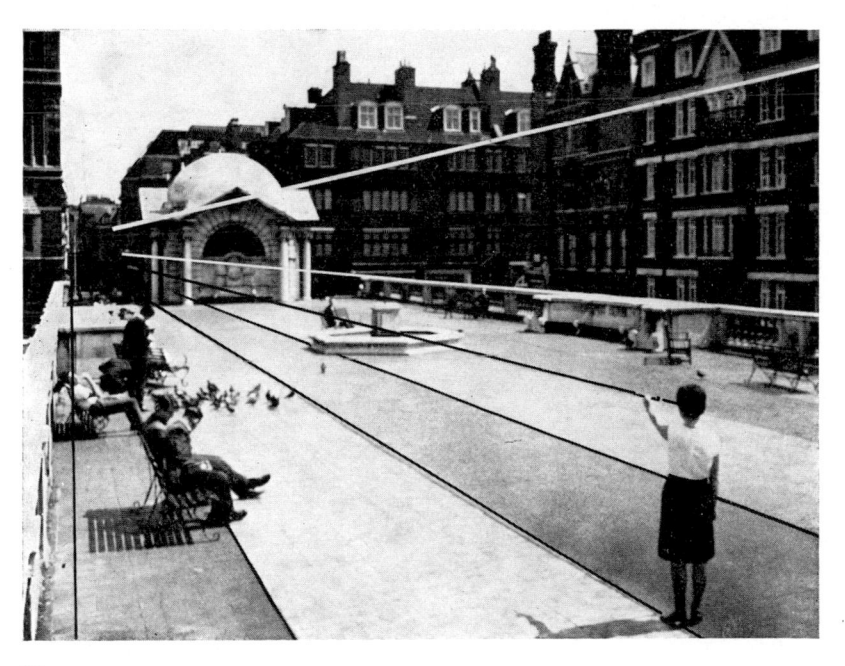

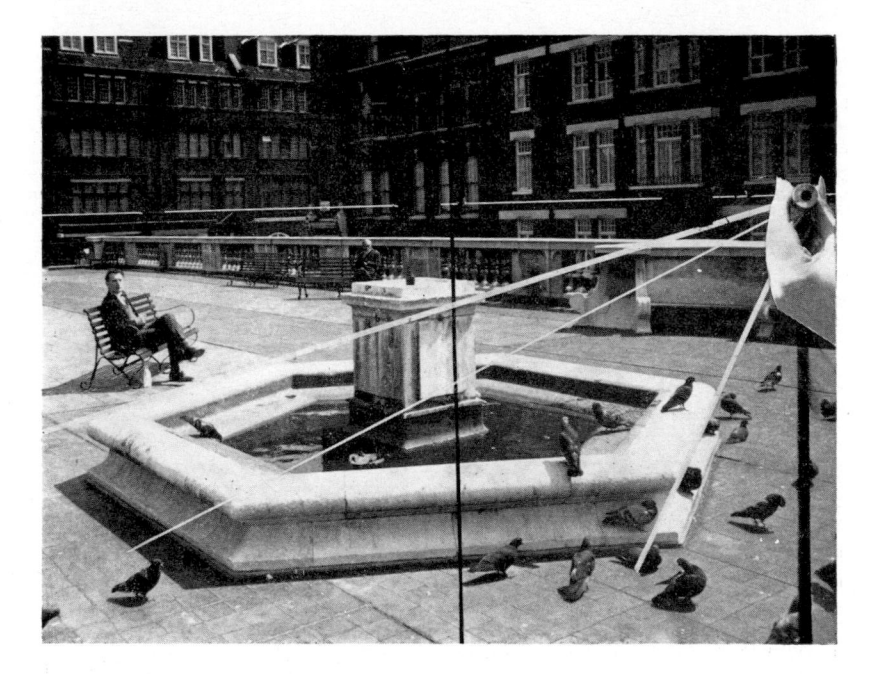

4.0/ The Vanishing Point.

4.1/ In perspective straight parallel lines apparently converge to a point. This occurs on a further imaginary parallel line projected from the eye of the Observer. Seen end-on, the section of this line appears as a point (like the end of a pointing pencil), that therefore occurs where all these parallel lines meet. This is called the Vanishing Point.

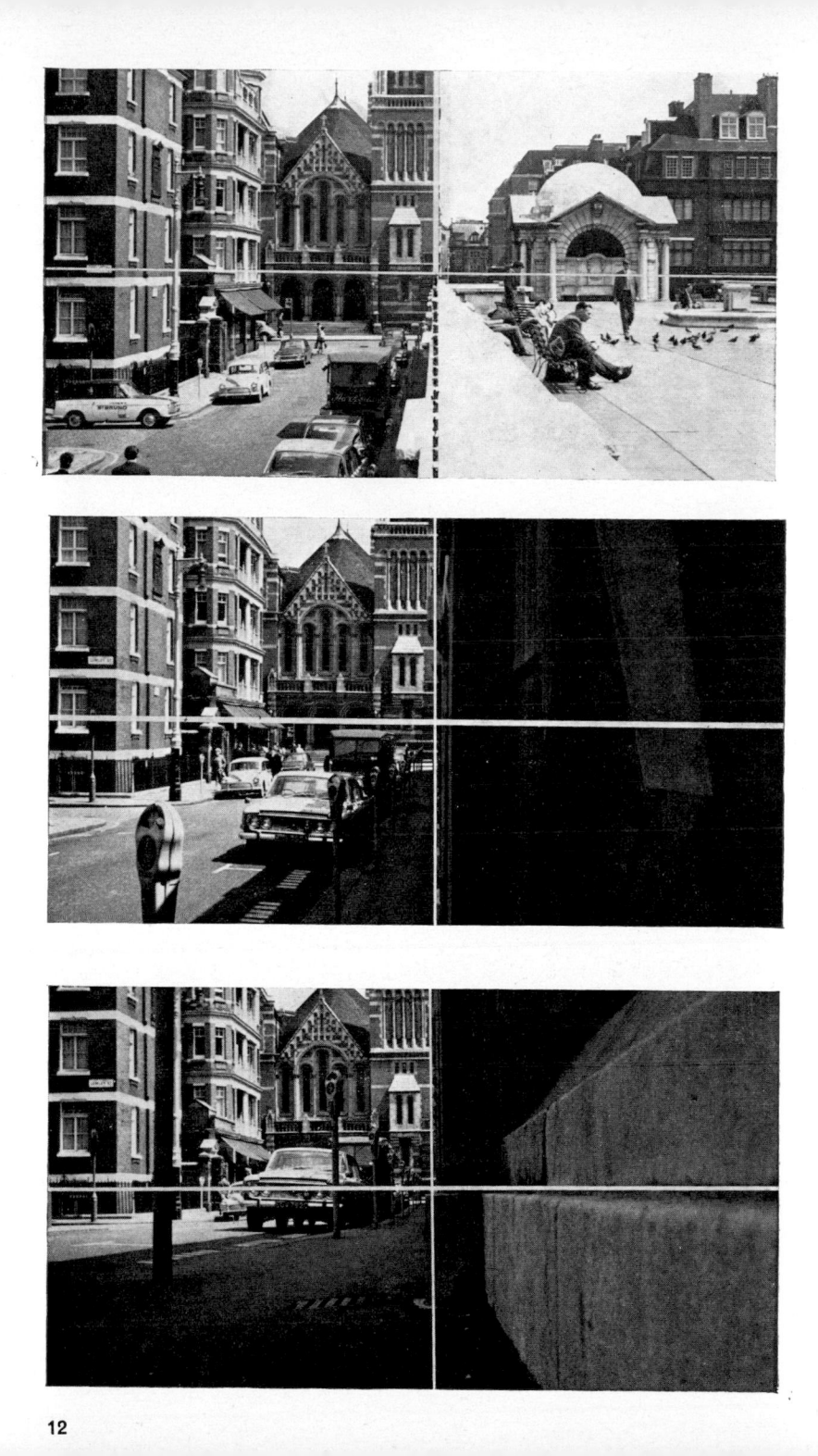

5.0/ The Eye Level.

5.1/ All equal heights above the Eye Level diminish in distance to zero at infinity and similarly all depths below the Eye Level diminish to zero. Thus all *horizontal* lines (joining the tops of equal heights) converge on the Eye Level, and horizontal *parallel* lines meet at a Vanishing Point on the Eye Level. It follows that the ground, if it is flat, cannot rise above the Eye Level and so the horizon (not necessarily the sky-line where there are hills, trees or buildings), is always at the Eye Level, and thus depends upon the height of the Observer above the ground. (This ignores the indiscernable lowering of the horizon due to the curvature of the Earth down and away from the Observer).

5.2/ Parallel lines that are not horizontal meet at a Vanishing Point above or below the Eye Level. This still obeys the rule that it is on a further imaginary parallel line from the eye (see 4.1 and 7.1).

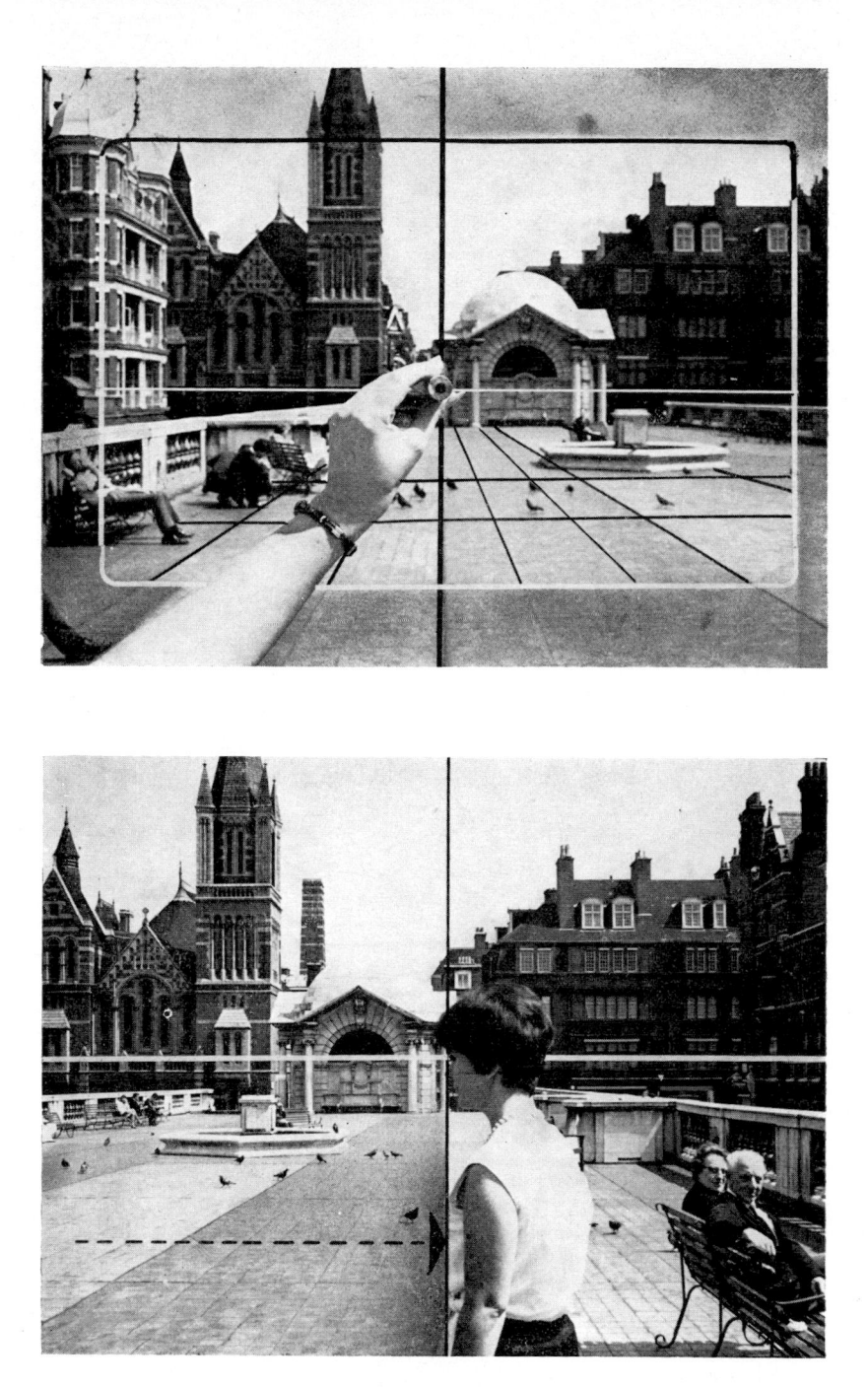

6.0/ The Vanishing Point on the Picture Plane.

6.1/ Parallel lines converge on the Vanishing Point where the parallel line from the Observer (4.1) cuts the Picture Plane. If the Observer and the parallel lines are stationary the Vanishing Point does NOT move.

6.2/ If the Observer *moves* right or left, or up or down, the Vanishing Point *moves* with him, and appears on the *new* Picture Plane on the parallel line from the new position. As he moves down, the Eye Level and Vanishing Point *and* the Picture Plane move down with him, e.g. as 5.1.

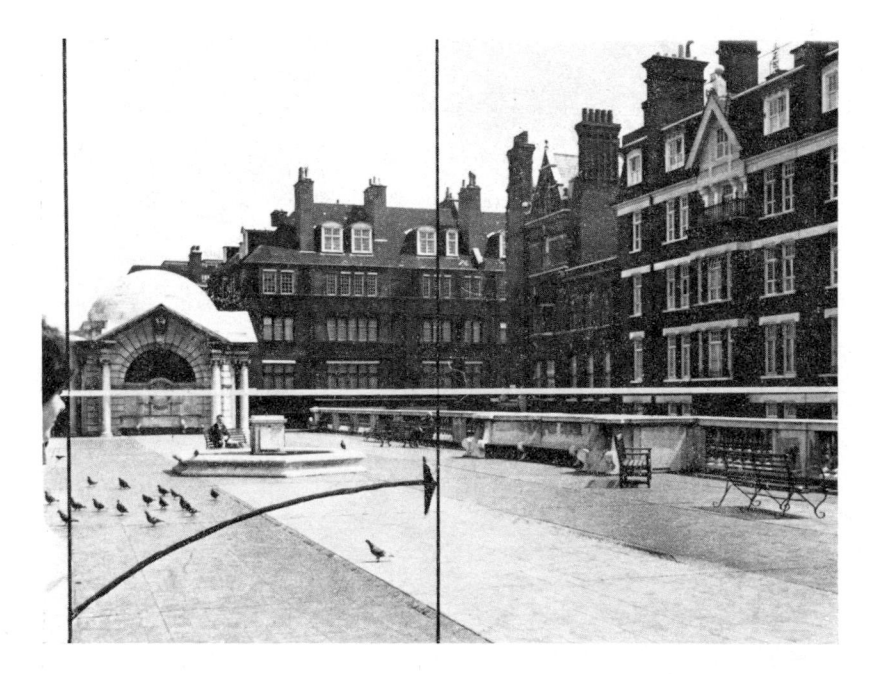

6.3/ When the Observer stays on the same spot but *turns*, the Vanishing Point still remains stationary, but as the Picture Plane, which is at right angles to the line of vision, *turns* with him—the position of the Vanishing Point *appears* to move across the turning Picture Plane.

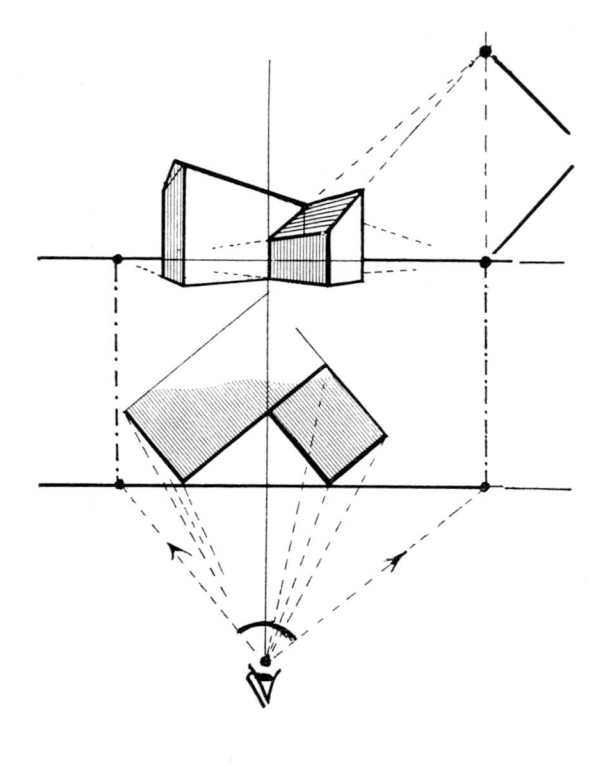

7.0/ The Vertical Picture Plane.

7.1/ When setting up a perspective, the Vanishing Point for parallel lines is established by drawing the line parallel to those lines from the eye of the Observer to cut the Picture Plane, for horizontal lines only, on the horizon or Eye Level.

7.2/ In the special case when the lines to be drawn are parallel to the Picture Plane itself, then the parallel line projected from the eye is also parallel to the Picture Plane and so it cannot cut the Picture Plane. The drawn lines have no Vanishing Point on the Picture Plane and must be drawn parallel.

16

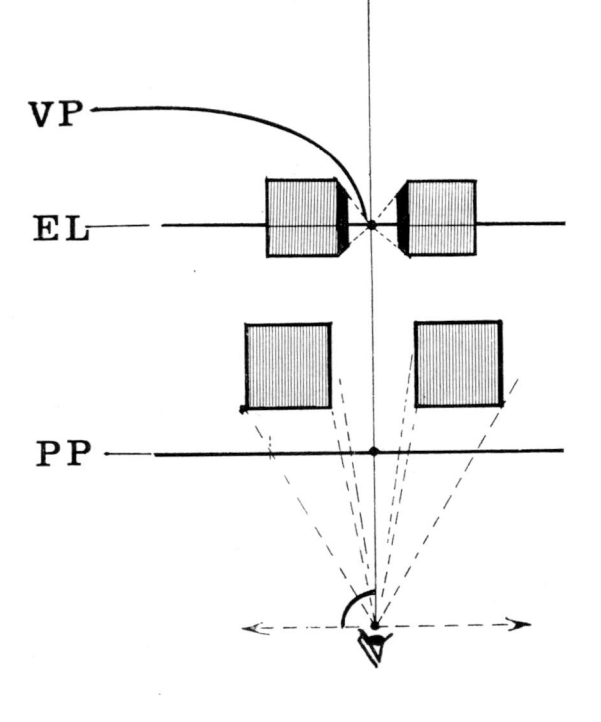

7.3/ Thus, on a vertical Picture Plane all verticals—by definition parallel—are drawn vertical. This accords with our sense of balance and gravity and thus a vertical Picture Plane is most commonly used. It is most suitable for architectural subjects and is used in both the parallel and oblique perspective methods here.

7.4/ In photography, if the camera is tilted up or down, then the resultant converging vertical lines can be most disturbing.

7.5/ Some perspectives, especially aerial views, do need a tilted Picture Plane to ensure that everything is included in the Cone of Vision. As this calls for another Vanishing Point for the verticals that are no longer parallel with the Picture Plane, the setting up is complicated and so has no place in these rapid methods.

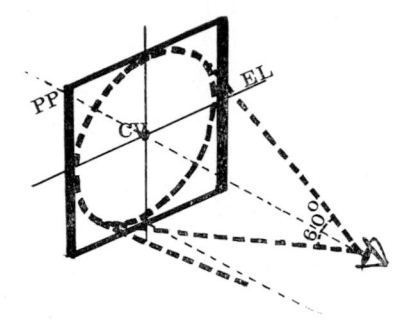

8.0/ The Cone of Vision

8.1/ To avoid distortions when viewing the resultant perspective the image produced on the Picture Plane is limited by the Cone of Vision.

8.2/ The Cone of Vision attempts to define the maximum area that can be appreciated from a static viewpoint. This is determined by the distance from the Picture Plane at which the area can be appreciated as a whole.

8.3/ The angle of the Cone is often given as a nominal 60° with the eye at the apex; the optimum size of drawing being taken as the square that is tangental to the Cone—that is to the circular section on the vertical Picture Plane. In practice the drawing is *a smaller section that is contained within this square (see page 33).*

8.4/ The Centre of Vision bisects the Eye Level at the centre of this square.

8.5/ The area of the view seen (as though through this square), increases as the depth increases.

8.6/ When setting up a perspective, there is often a temptation to add a little more at the edges by increasing the view outside the acceptable Cone of Vision, but in a perspective drawing such an increased view requires a closer viewpoint to avoid the resultant distortions. At so close a distance it may be difficult to view the picture as a whole. It follows that the Observer has to move back to a more acceptable viewpoint, and not being the original one used when setting up, the resultant distortions are then apparent. Such distortions are particularly noticeable at the edges of a picture, and not least, they give rise to an exaggeration of the sense of depth.

8.7/ These distortions are readily noticeable in photography in small contact prints which cannot be viewed from the necessary close viewpoint, but when enlarged they do give a much more convincing illusion of reality. So it is that it is often preferable to have a smaller Cone of Vision to reduce further the likelihood of distortion.

8.8/ In spite of the basis upon which the Cone of Vision is decided, some extension outside is possible, for if the perspective is otherwise consistent the eye can tolerate a degree of distortion. For example, tall buildings especially when isolated, may appear outside the 60° Cone when the resultant distortions enhance a sensation of height. A skilled draughtsman, able to maintain such a consistency, can sometimes emphasise the spatial effects by judiciously using such distortions.

8.9/ That we can accept these distortions is an illustration of what psychologists term *constancy*. For example, a moving form does not seem to change its shape and size as it turns, or advances or recedes. Although the image on the retina is continuously changing, it appears constant. In the case of perspective it may be seen that as long as the images presented are reasonably consistent with our perceptions of known forms, and any distortions are consistent with one another, the sense of reality is maintained. The simple proof of this is that any picture may be looked at from an oblique angle with little loss of perspective or realism. If this were not so we would all need individual television and cinema screens immediately in front of us.

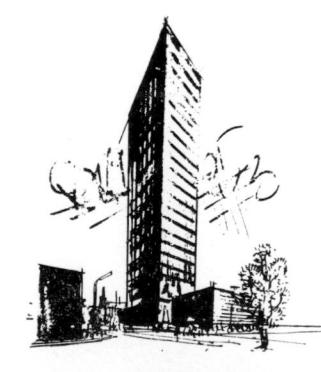

9.0/ Parallel perspective

9.1/ Uses and advantages

a) Parallel perspective is the simplest method of setting up.

b) It may be developed from drawn plans and elevations; from plan and vertical dimensions, or vice versa; or from dimensions only as in the methods in this book.

c) It is particularly suited to the rectangular forms and spaces found in architecture, but any point, oblique line or free form may be plotted.

9.2/ When setting up for rectilinear forms and spaces:

a) the central line of vision from the eye is aligned parallel to the horizontal receding lines,

b) the vertical Picture Plane, is set at right angles to this line of vision (3.3) it follows that:

c) all verticals are drawn vertical (7.2 and 7.3)

d) all horizontal lines parallel to the Picture Plane (that is at right angles to the receding planes) are drawn horizontal (7.2)

c) the centre of Vision is at the centre of the square elevation of the Cone of vision on the Picture Plane, and because it is on a line from the Viewpoint parallel to the horizontal receding lines, it coincides with their Vanishing Point on the Eye Level (8.1; 8.2; 8.3).

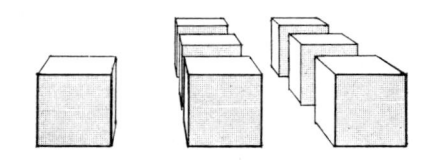

9.3/ Some observers, whilst able to accept the correctness of parallel vertical lines, find difficulty in seeing that all horizontal lines parallel to the Picture Plane are drawn horizontally and so *correspond* with our normal perception. The confusion arises from the fact that all horizontal straight lines must recede from the Observer and seem to converge at a distance. The reason for the correctness of the construction is that the Picture Plane itself and the horizontal lines drawn on it are parallel to such receding lines and from the Viewpoint, *both* sets appear to converge at the same angle. It follows that a square parallel to the Picture Plane is drawn, but not seen as a square, however far it is off-centre. This may be shown to be so by turning the illustration through 90° when any offending horizontals become vertical and immediately appear satisfactory.

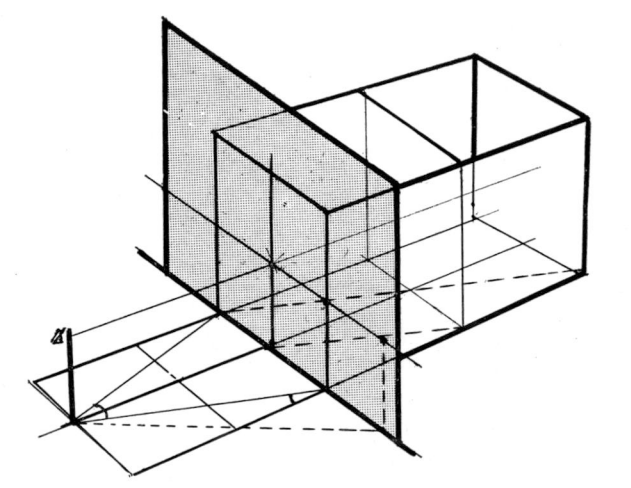

10.0/ Rapid Parallel perspective.

10.1/ Basis for setting up
This method is based on a cube grid with one side being that square on the Picture Plane which is tangental to the Cone of Vision (8.3).

10.2/ The diagram shows the Viewpoint is one square back from the Picture Plane to give an acceptable Cone of Vision—53° 20′. This point is plotted by drawing the diagonal of a double square—26° 40′—from the side of the cube at the Picture Plane to where it cuts the Central Line of Vision. (8.1 ; 8.3 and 8.4).

10.3/ This same diagonal gives the Vanishing Point for all lines at the same angle—that is all diagonals of double squares in plan. This is to permit large scale drawings with *no outside* constructions. (Note: the construction to give Vanishing Point for 45° diagonals outside square, *see next page*).

10.4/ Any scale may be applied to the grid and any point may be plotted within it—and lines or forms may be set up (3.4).

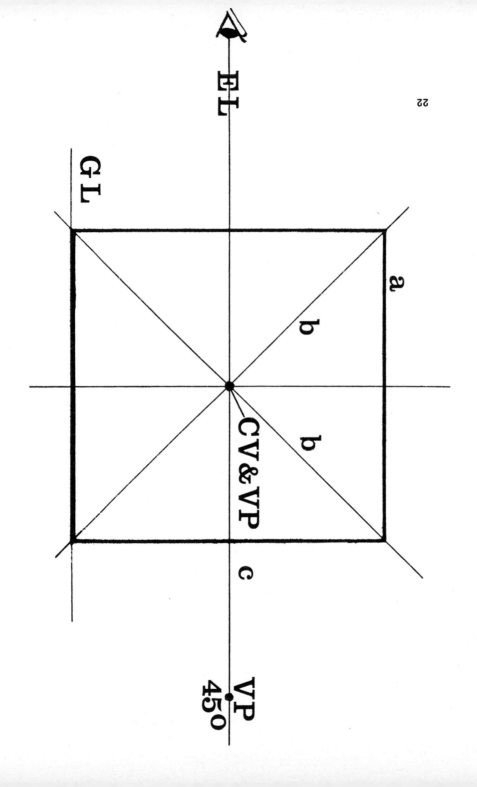

EL

GL

22

a

b

b

CV&VP

c

VP
450

Procedure to set up a space grid based on a cube:

a) DRAW A SQUARE TO SCALE TO GIVE DESIRED SIZE OF DRAWING (as large as is practicable). The bottom line is the ground or floor at the Picture Plane and is called the Ground Line.

b) DRAW THE TWO DIAGONALS. Where they meet is the Centre of Vision and the Vanishing Point for all lines receding from the Observer from points on the Picture Plane, at right angles to the Picture Plane. The diagonals therefore define the edges of the cube extended to infinity, or in effect to the Eye Level on the horizon.

c) DRAW THE HORIZONTAL EYE LEVEL THROUGH THE CENTRE OF VISION

d) MARK THE VANISHING POINT FOR THE 45° DIAGONALS OF THE SQUARE PLAN OF THE EYE LEVEL AT HALF THE WIDTH OF THE SQUARE OUTSIDE THE SQUARE (note 10.3 above).

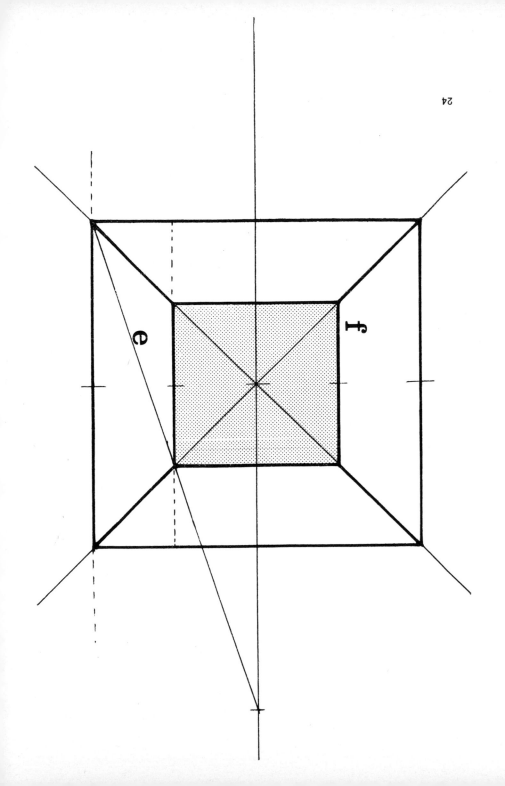

e

f

e) JOIN A CORNER OF THE SQUARE ELEVATION ON THE GROUND LINE AT THE PICTURE PLANE TO THE 45° VANISHING POINT. This represents the diagonal of the square plan.

f) CONSTRUCT A SQUARE IN ELEVATION WITH ITS CORNER AT THE POINT WHERE THIS DIAGONAL LINE CUTS THE BASE LINE OF THE 'RECEDING' PLANE OF THE CUBE. This is the far side of a cube and being twice the distance of the Picture Plane from the observer, scales half the front elevation. (The area of section is therefore four times the front square, and at times this plane may be used to set up an elevation and project forward. The limit of the Cone of Vision being twice linear the rear elevation).

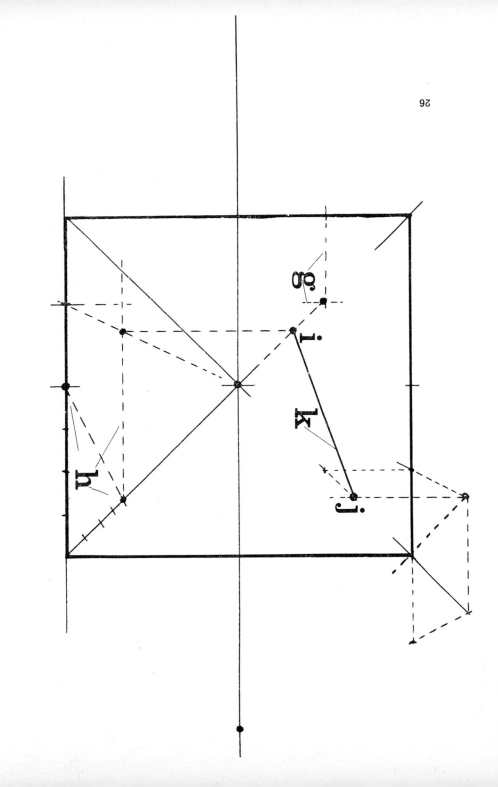

g) SCALE HEIGHTS AND WIDTHS ON THE PICTURE PLANE (OR, at $\frac{1}{2}$ SCALE ON THE PLANE AT REAR OF CUBE) LINES DRAWN THROUGH THESE POINTS TO VANISHING POINT AT CENTRE OF VISION TO GIVE DIMENSIONS RECEDING TO INFINITY.

h) SCALE DEPTHS ALONG GROUND LINE OF SQUARE ELEVATION AND JOINT TO 45° VANISHING POINT. THE POINTS WHERE THESE DIAGONALS CUT THE BASE OF RECEDING PLANE GIVE THE CORRECT DEPTH IN PERSPECTIVE (as **e** above). All points vertically of horizontally from this point are at the same distance from the Picture Plane or from the Observer.

i) Any point in the grid may be plotted from given dimensions by vertical and horizontal construction.

j) Points can be plotted in front of the Picture Plane, if they fall within the square.

k) A line in any direction can be plotted between two points.

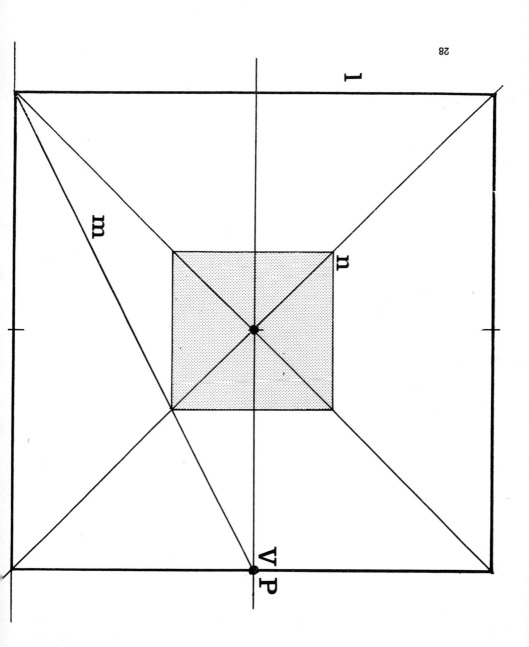

l

m

n

v P

l) When a large drawing is required it is often convenient not to have a Vanishing Point outside the perspective itself. The following construction permits this and at the same time makes it easier to develop a perspective by using the Vanishing Point of diagonals of the double square in plan that occurs on the side of the square (see 8.3).

m) JOIN THE SIDE OF THE SQUARE FROM GROUND LINE ON THE PICTURE PLANE TO THE VANISHING POINT ON THE SIDE OF THE SQUARE, i. e. with the diagonal of a double square in perspective.

n) CONSTRUCT A SQUARE IN ELEVATION WITH ITS CORNER AT THE POINT WHERE THIS LINE CUTS THE BASE LINE OF THE 'RECEDING' PLANE. This is, by construction, the far side of the double cube, and being three times the distance from the observer as is the Picture Plane, scales ⅓ the front elevation. At times it may be convenient to set up an elevation on the far plane and project it forward. (The limit of the Cone of Vision being three times linear of the rear elevation).

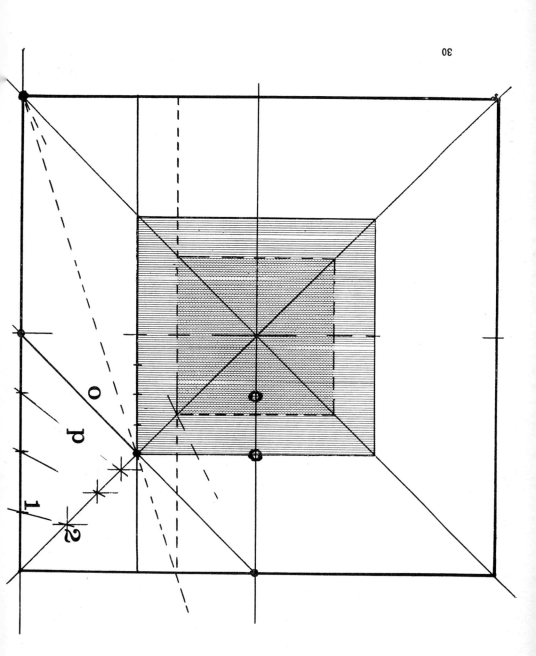

o) IN THE SAME WAY, THE MID POINT OF THE BASE LINE WHEN JOINED TO THIS VANISHING POINT GIVES A DEPTH OF ONE CUBE. This far side scales $\frac{1}{2}$ the scale at the Picture Plane. This plane may be a convenient position to set up elevation and gives four times the area of front plane. This, of course, coincides with the cube drawing as set up with the 45° diagonal (**e** above).

p) THE DEPTH SCALE ON THE PICTURE PLANE IS NOW TAKEN AS HALF THE VERTICAL AND HORIZONTAL SCALE. (HEIGHTS AND WIDTHS AS BEFORE ARE SCALED ON THE PICTURE PLANE ETC) **g–i** and **j** as above still apply.
(By observation it may be seen that it follows that a Vanishing Point **o** half way between the Centre of Vision and side of square may be used with a $\frac{1}{4}$ full scale depth scale, and similarly a point **o** half way again towards the Centre of Vision permits the use of an $\frac{1}{8}$ full scale depth scale. These scales are used for subjects in depth).

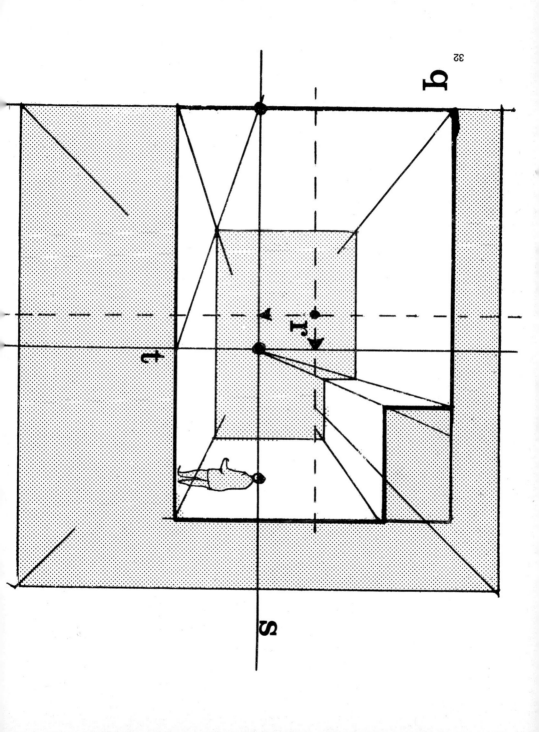

32

Setting up Parallel Perspective from dimensions

The interdependent heights and widths of a section to the drawing, and where the Viewpoint and Eye Level occur, must first be determined ; after which, neither plan nor elevations other than the relevant dimensions are necessary for this setting up procedure—a dimensioned sketch plan is sufficient.

q) DRAW THE SECTION REQUIRED. The scale is determined by the size of the drawing and dimensions it must represent. The section shown can be vertical or horizontal in the following constructions. (Turn the diagram around to see this.) The section can also be seen as in a Plan for a 'Bird's eye view'. Note that the shaded area is in practice not shown.

r) THE CENTRE OF VISION CAN BE OFF-CENTRE OF THIS SECTION—BOTH VERTICALLY AND HORIZONTALLY.

s) DECIDE EYE LEVEL. Normally 5' 0" standing ; or 3' 0"—4' 0" sitting ; or any other height required.

t) DECIDE LINE OF VISION IN PLAN THAT PERMITS THE REQUIRED FEATURES TO BE SEEN. This should be central or as near central axis of plan as possible to avoid 'looking out of the corner of the eye'. *(see plan on next page).*

33

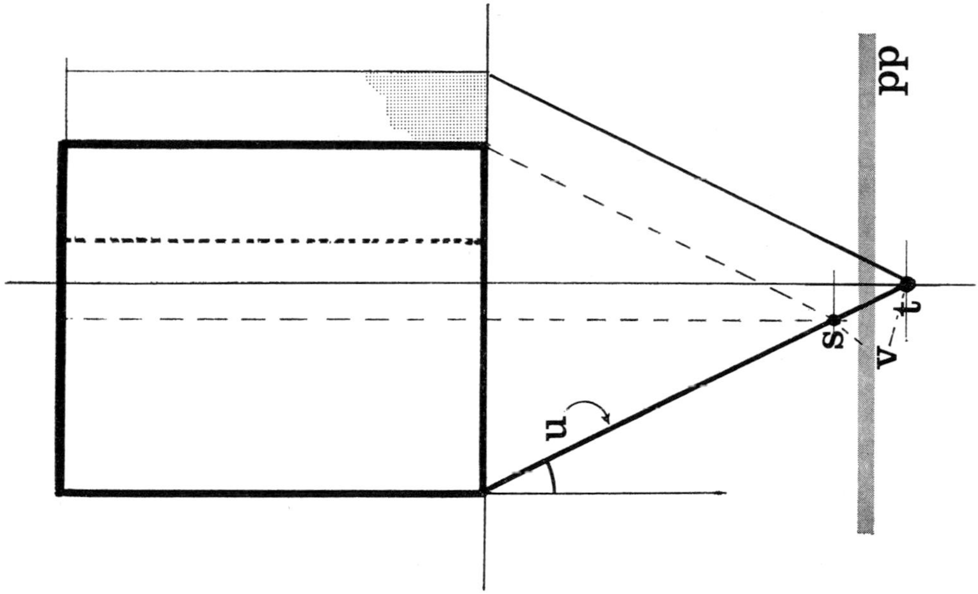
pp
u
s
v
t

The position of the Viewpoint is critical in deciding what the resultant perspective will show but it is not used in the actual setting-up procedure.

The Observer's Viewpoint is shown on plan.

u) DRAW A DIAGONAL OF A DOUBLE SQUARE (26° 40') FROM THE **FURTHEST** POINT HEIGHT OR WIDTH OF THE SECTION FROM THE CENTRE OF VISION TO WHERE IT CUTS THE CENTRAL LINE OF VISION (here it is width in plan). This illustrates that any movement of the Observer from the central point as in **s** and **t** requires that he moves back to include everything in the Cone of Vision. This means that the effective square on the Picture Plane is larger than the section to be drawn (8.0).

In moving back to include forms in the foreground, the Viewpoint may fall outside an enclosing wall, when the resultant perspective would be an overlong space. But if the Cone of Vision is exceeded to include more information it gives rise to distortions and a similar exaggeration of the length (8.6).

However, a Viewpoint from not too far outside a space produces a perspective acceptable as one from inside. This is because the eye constantly scans a wider area than is seen from the the static Viewpoint.

v) DECIDE BETWEEN THIS DISTANT VIEWPOINT THAT INCLUDES FORMS IN THE FORE-GROUND AND THAT NEAR VIEWPOINT WHICH SHOWS THE SPATIAL RELATIONSHIPS AS SEEN FROM WITHIN. This decision determines where the Picture Plane is placed, or in the procedure here, what the dimensions in depth are.

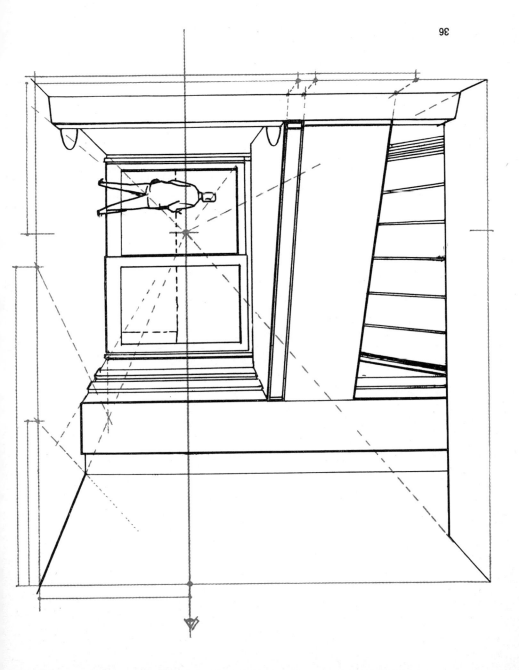

EXAMPLE OF PARALLEL PERSPECTIVE.

This illustration shows all the construction necessary to produce an interior perspective.

House in Kensington Place by Tom Kay, ARIBA

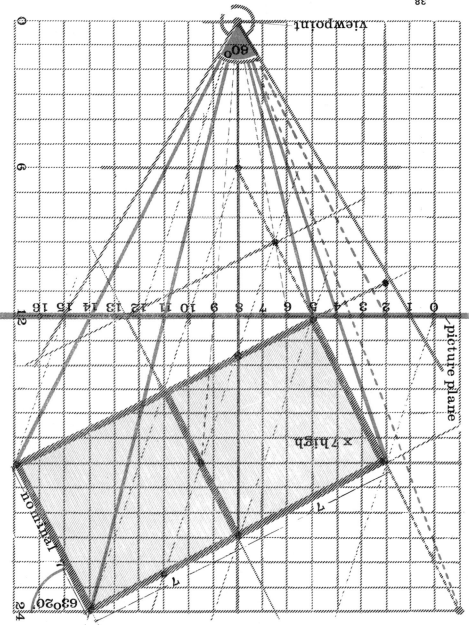

viewpoint

60°

picture plane

0 1 2 3 4 5 6 7 8 9 10 11 12 13 14 15 16

x 7 high

7 long

63°20'

6

12

24

0

11.0/ Rapid Oblique perspective: basis for setting up.

11.1/ This method of oblique perspective gives a useful alternative to parallel perspective. The constructions are within the page and in this way the size of the drawing is not limited.

11.2/ This method rationalizes the setting up of a grid based upon a double cube 7 x 7 x 7 [x 14] set at an angle of 63° 20′/26° 40′ to a vertical Picture Plane. In plan this aligns the diagonal of the double square parallel to the Picture Plane.

11.3/ The plan shows the fixed position of the Observer and the Centre of Vision in relation to a Picture Plane and the double-cube space grid. This relationship gives verticles and Vanishing Points that occur above fixed points on a horizontal **0–16** setting-up scale.

11.4/ The horizontal units **0–16** of the setting-up scale provide an oblique space grid in perspective with the side of the units cube equalling **7** units.

11.5/ **16** to **7** is a fixed ratio, but it will be seen that any multiple or scale may be applied to the resultant cube grid.

11.6/ The nominal cube of **7** units gives a consistent increase of the relative height to square plan of approximately 4%. This is to simplify the setting up procedure but, being compatible with our normal exaggeration of height, it cannot be detected in the final drawing. For those who require strict accuracy of dimensions, the height of the cube should scale 6.7081 horizontal setting-up units.

11.7/ The Observer is twelve units from the Picture Plane to give a 60° 'Cone of Vision' at the Picture Plane at 7 units from the Centre of Vision.

11.8/ In plan the Viewpoint and Centre of Vision are fixed with regard to the vertical Picture Plane and the space grid, but within the grid any points may be plotted.

11.9/ The Eye Level is not fixed and is a factor when choosing the scale for the drawing.

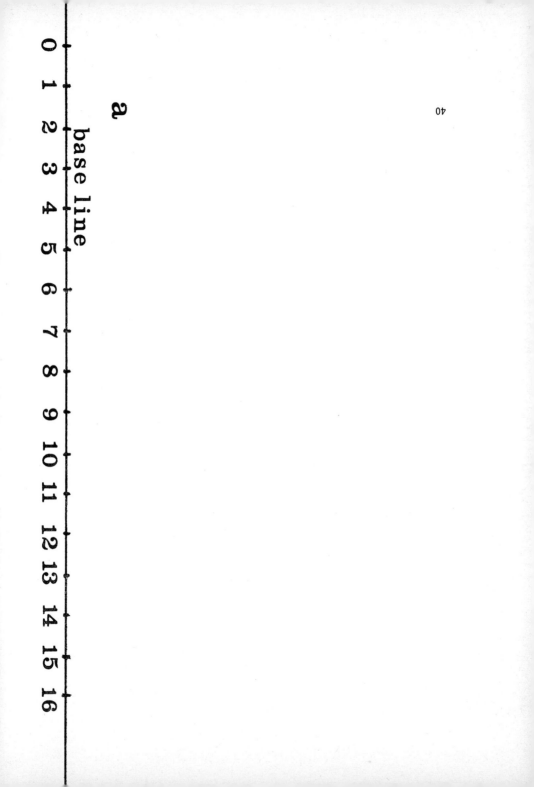

a

base line

0 1 2 3 4 5 6 7 8 9 10 11 12 13 14 15 16

40

Procedure to set up a space grid based on a double cube.

a) DRAW HORIZONTAL BASE LINE, AND MARK 0–16 UNITS. This gives full width of Picture Plane and may be as large as is practicable.

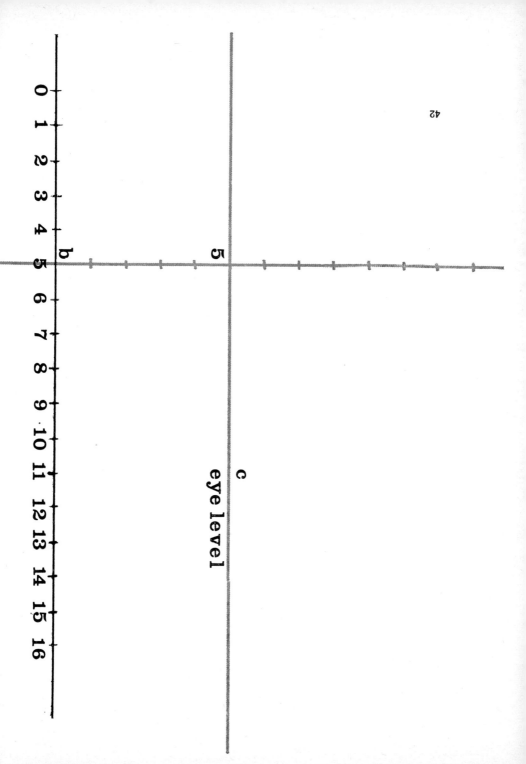

b) DRAW VERTICAL MEASURING LINE at **5**.

c) DRAW EYE LEVEL ACROSS FULL WIDTH OF DRAWING AT PREDETERMINED HEIGHT ABOVE BASE LINE. Here for example, at **5**. The Eye Level can be at any height between 0 and 7 units.

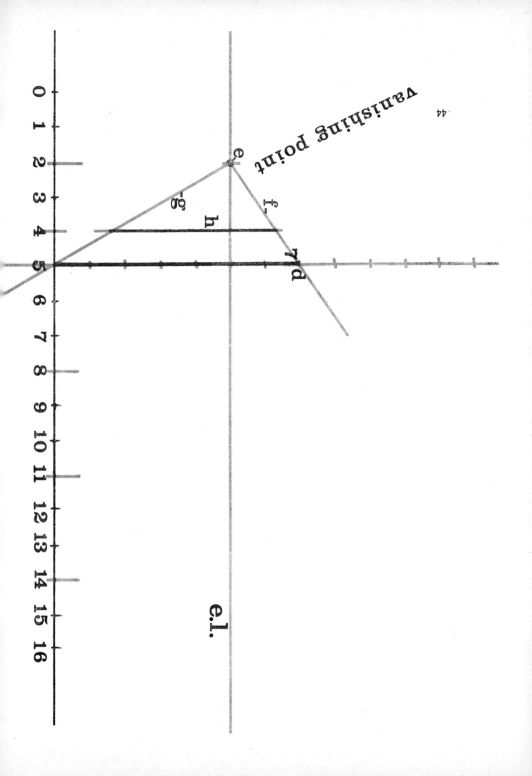

vanishing point

44

e.l.

d) MARK FULL HEIGHT OF CUBE ON VERTICAL **5–7** UNITS ABOVE BASE LINE. (here it is 2 units above Eye Level). This represents front corner of near cube.

e) MARK VANISHING POINT ON EYE LEVEL AT VERTICAL **2**.

f) JOIN THE TOP OF VERTICAL **5** TO VANISHING POINT AT **2**.

g) JOIN BASE OF **5** TO VANISHING POINT AT **2**.

h) DRAW VERTICAL **4** TO CONNECT THE LAST TWO CONVERGING LINES **f** and **g**. This represents the receding left hand square side of the cube. The far height at vertical **4** scales $\frac{2}{3}$ the height at vertical **5**.

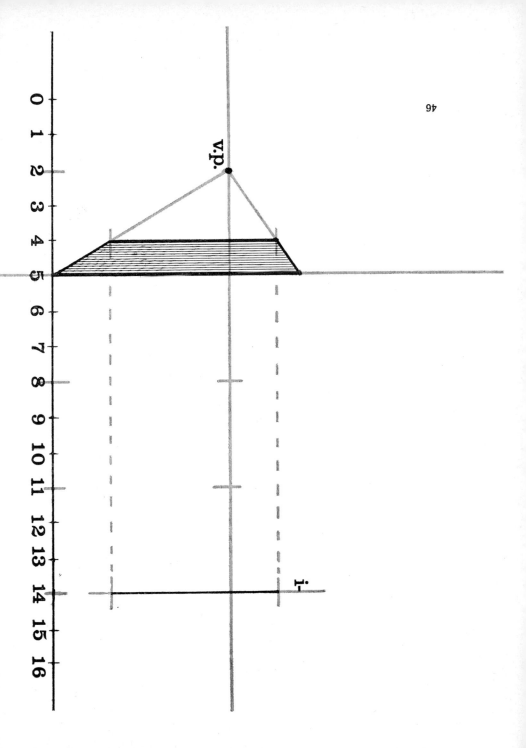

j) DRAW VERTICAL AT **14** AND PROJECT HORIZONTALLY THE HEIGHT OF **4** ACROSS TO VERTICAL **14**. This height represents right hand corner of far cube and is also $\frac{2}{3}$ vertical height **5**. The project lines follow diagonal of double square base parallel to the Picture Plane and give $\frac{2}{3}$ horizontal scale on Picture Plane (Base Line). This plane may be used to develop the drawing in depth.

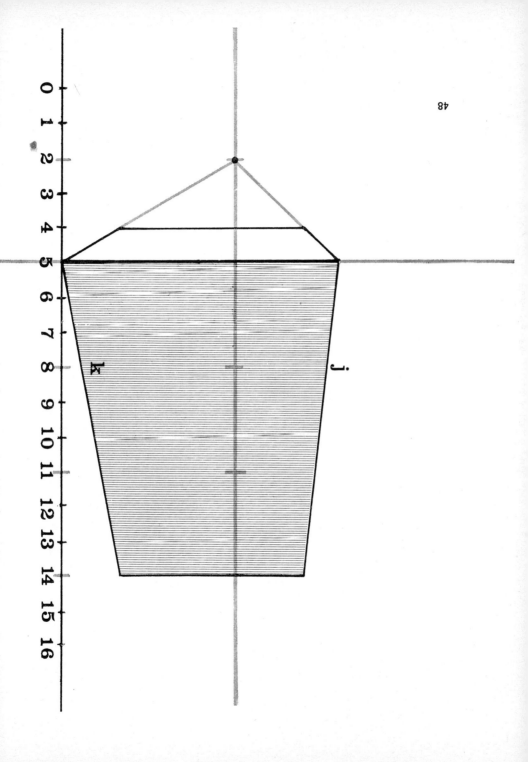

j) JOIN TOP OF VERTICAL **5** TO TOP OF VERTICAL **14**

k) JOIN BOTTOM OF VERTICAL **5** TO BOTTOM OF VERTICAL **14**. This represents receding double square, and both exterior faces are now drawn.

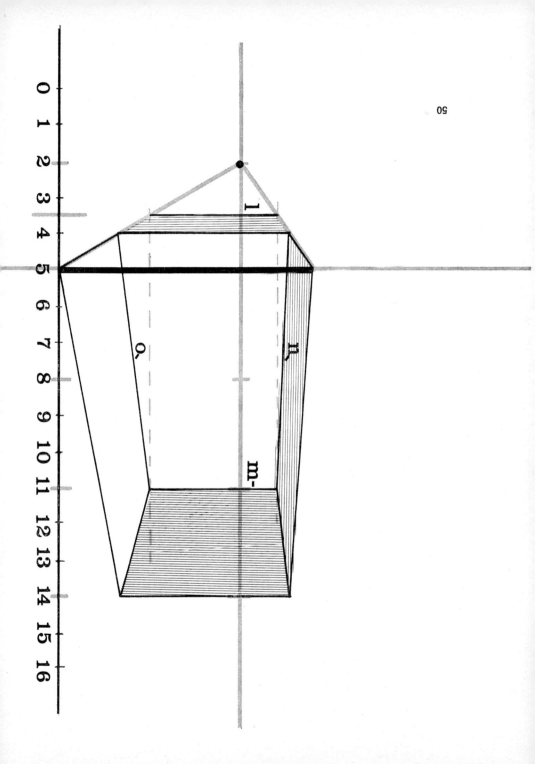

l) DRAW VERTICAL AT $3\frac{1}{2}$ TO JOIN TOP AND BOTTOM CONVERGING LINES (AS DESCRIBED IN **f** AND **g** ABOVE.) This defines a second square in the same plane as the left hand receding square side of near cube. This height scales $\frac{1}{2}$ height at **5**.

m) DRAW VERTICAL AT **11** AND HORIZONTALLY PROJECT THE HEIGHT OF $3\frac{1}{2}$ ACROSS TO THIS VERTICAL **11**. This represents far corner of double cube and, of course, also scales $\frac{1}{2}$ height at **5**. The projection lines are a further diagonal of the double square parallel to the Picture Plane, scaling $\frac{1}{2}$ scale of Picture Plane and again may be used to develop the drawing in depth.

n) JOIN TOP OF VERTICAL **4** TO TOP OF VERTICAL **11**.

o) JOIN BOTTOM OF VERTICAL **4** TO BOTTOM OF VERTICAL **11**. These define the far side of the double cube and all six sides are drawn.

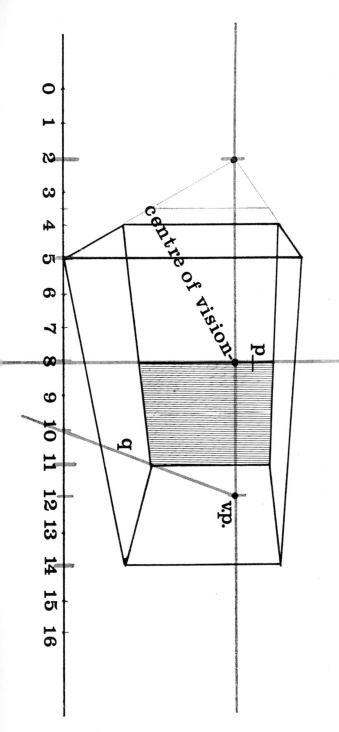

centre of vision

p

q

vp.

0 1 2 3 4 5 6 7 8 9 10 11 12 13 14 15 16

To divide a double cube

p) DIVIDE THE REAR PLANE OF THE DOUBLE CUBE INTO TWO SQUARES BY A VERTICAL AT **8**. Where this vertical cuts the Eye Level is the Centre of Vision.

(Note: Basic setting-up of verticals, at intervals of 3 units, 2, 5, 8, 11, 14).

q) JOIN POINT **10** ON BASE LINE TO POINT ON EYE LEVEL AT VERTICAL **12**. This passes through bottom of far corner of far cube and represents the 45° diagonal of the far square in plan.

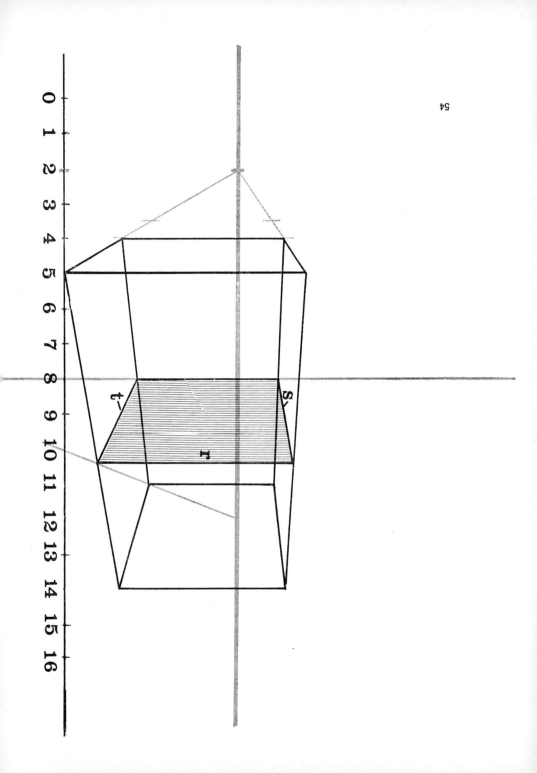

r) ERECT A VERTICAL FROM THE POINT WHERE THIS DIAGONAL CUTS BOTTOM CON-VERGING LINE TO TOP CONVERGING LINE. This divides the front plane into two squares.

s) JOIN TOP OF THIS VERTICAL TO TOP OF VERTICAL **8**.

t) JOIN BOTTOM OF THIS VERTICAL TO BOTTOM OF VERTICAL **8**. These represent the dividing square between the two cubes and all surfaces of both cubes are now drawn.

(Note: Only the actual lines needed to represent the double cube need be drawn).

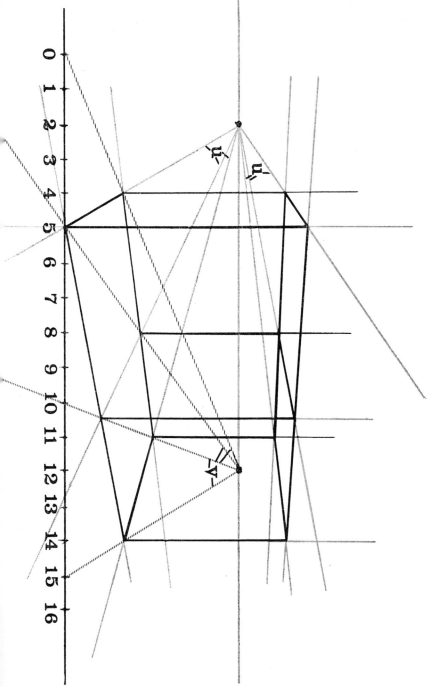

To develop cube grid in depth

u) PROJECT LINES FROM VANISHING POINT AT **2** THROUGH TOP AND BOTTOM OF HEIGHTS AT **4**, **8** AND **11**. (Note: Lines **s**, **t** and then **r**, may be constructed on this basis).

v) JOIN POINTS **0**, **5**, **10** AND **15** ON BASE LINE TO POINT **12** ON EYE LEVEL. These lines represent the 45° diagonals of squares on plan.

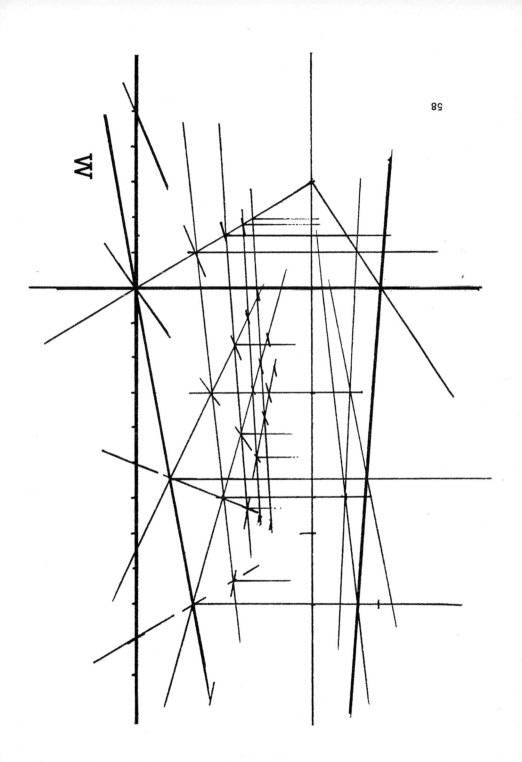

W

w) WHERE THESE DIAGONALS CUT THE SQUARES IN PERSPECTIVE CONSTRUCT FURTHER SQUARES IN PERSPECTIVE. Points can be plotted both behind and in front of double cube and the perspective developed rapidly in depth. In practice only those lines needed to define subject need be drawn.

This is the basic grid for setting up. Any scale may be applied to the cube grid if the 16:7 ratio is maintained.

Any point may be scaled in depth by dividing the base line to the required scale.

The Diagonals cut both directions of the receding square plan at the same depths. (See alternative methods under **x** and **x**´ below).

Two diagonals determine the distance between points in either direction.

12.0/ To set up points from given dimensions. These notes allow development from sketch plans and elevations that provide the proposed dimensions.

12.1/ The construction can, of course, be mirrored left to right (*see page 72*).

12.2/ The Eye Level can be at any height between zero, on the Base Line, up to 7 units maximum (one cube high). If the Eye Level is low the plan construction can be skied for easier reading (compare by inverting and see alternative II below).

12.3/ The Maximum height above the Eye Level is a further 7 units—giving a total of 14 units within the Cone of Vision (two cubes high are the Picture Plane).

12.4/ The Maximum width is determined by the face of the receding double cube. This can be extended left and right within the 14 unit Cone of Vision—Verticals **1** to **15** inclusive—to give a total of three squares in length. The placing of the cube grid is determined to give the simplest plotting of points that do not occur on the face of the cube grid. With a plan this can be found by a tracing over showing Cone of Vision and the Picture Plane.

12.5/ Heights are constructed in two ways—see **z**, example **b**. As for the cube grid, measure at vertical **5**, project back to vertical **4**, project across to vertical **14**. The line joining the heights on verticals **5** and **14** is the required height in perspective. Heights at intermediate positions may be established by scaling on the Picture Plane by projection from vanishing points **2** or **12**.

12.6/ Measurements *in depth* are constructed from the established depth scale along the Base Line. Points and required lengths are scaled and when projected back as diagonals to the Vanishing Point at **12** cut the square grid or other parallel lines to the correct dimensions in perspective (*see* **z** *and* **z'**)

12.7/ When developing perspective in depth, dimensions may be scaled half vertical and horizontal scales on the Picture Plane on the diagonal of the double square parallel to the Picture Plane, that is in the plane through verticals $3\frac{1}{2}$ and **11**. (Similarly $\frac{2}{3}$ scale in plane through verticals **4** and **14**; *see i and l*).

12.8/ The actual size of the scale used is not limited. It depends on the size of drawing and of the subject. It is determined by **1—4** above. When fixed the different horizontal and vertical scales are established (see **x** and **y** and **x'** and **y'** below). Points may now be plotted.

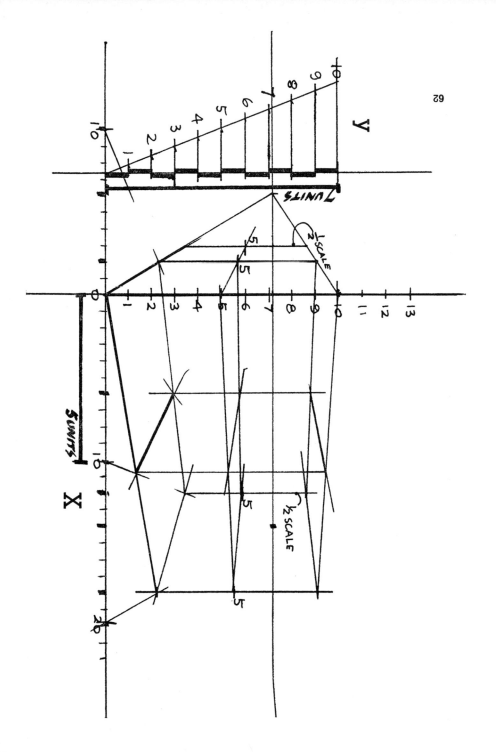

12.9/ There are two methods for establishing the different vertical and depth scale (5 above) :

Alternative I—to construct a 10 x 10 x 10 cube, grid suitable for decimal subdivision. This uses the Base Line units as a DEPTH SCALE and converts 7 vertical units into 10 HEIGHT SCALE units.

x) CONNECT POINTS **0–16** to VANISHING POINT **12** (45° diagonals) TO CUT BOTH SIDES OF THE SQUARE PLAN IN PERSPECTIVE INTO FIFTHS. HALF THIS SCALE GIVES A SCALE OF 10 WITH DECIMAL SUBDIVISIONS FOR THE CUBE. The height of the cube (7 units) also scales **10**.

y) DIVIDE **7** VERTICAL UNITS INTO **HEIGHT SCALE** of 10. This may be done geometrically or a useful permanent scale may be made for use with a standard sized unit (see page 83).

(Note that in the illustration, the conversion of the scale has made the Eye Level 7.2 units, and therefore it is necessary to establish a vertical scale before setting up a perspective).

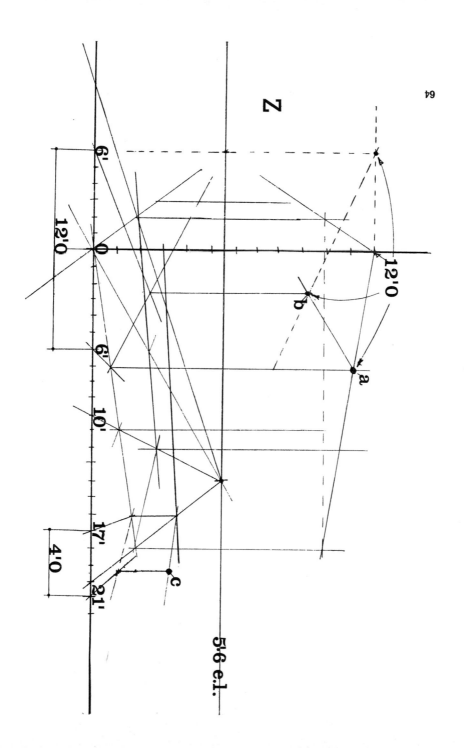

z) Determine the size of scale based on drawing, size and height and width of subject to be drawn.

PLOT POINTS FROM GIVEN DIMENSIONS. Examples presuming scales equal 1' per unit:

a) A point 6' from near corner and 12' high on front face of double cube.

b) A point 12' behind on the square plan of point **2**. (Note height taken from face of cube, point a, or from Picture Plane) (see **12.5**).

c) A point 4' in front of this face, 17' from near corner, 3' high.

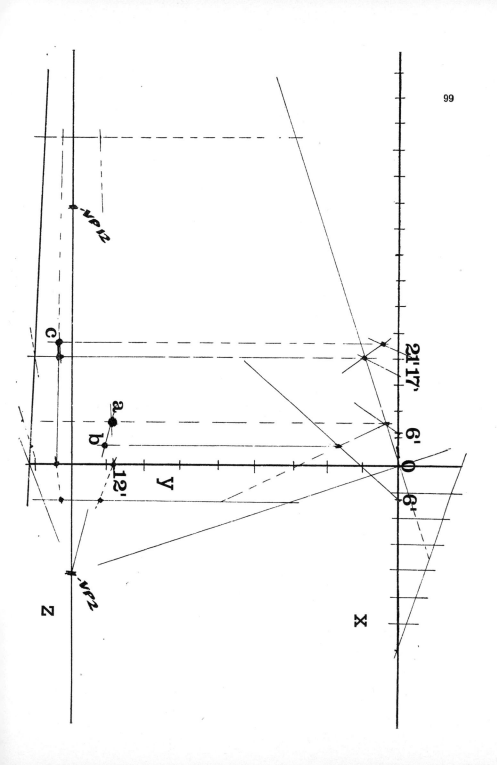

Alternative II—to construct a 7 x 7 x 7 cube grid.

This uses the Vertical Units as a HEIGHT SCALE and converts **5** Base Line units into 7 DEPTH SCALE units.

The Eye Level can be scaled immediately.

This diagram is reversed and inverted (turn around for comparison). Because the Eye Level is low, the scales are above for clarity when setting up. Note that when setting up (in both alternatives) the cube grid is not shown except for the plane that cuts the Picture Plane at Vertical **5**.

The alternative method now reads :

x¹) DIVIDE **5** BASE LINE UNITS INTO **DEPTH SCALE** OF 7. This may be done geometrically or a useful permanent scale may be made for use with a standard sized unit. (This does not replace setting up 1–16 Vertical scale).

CONNECT POINTS ON **DEPTH SCALE** TO VANISHING POINT **12** (45° diagonals) TO CUT BOTH SIDES OF SQUARE PLAN IN PERSPECTIVE AT THE CORRECT DISTANCE.

y¹) The Vertical units are used for the HEIGHT SCALE (with suitable subdivisions).

z¹) Determine the size of scale based on drawing size and of height, and width of subject to be drawn.

PLOT POINTS FROM GIVEN DIMENSIONS. Examples presuming scales equal 5' per unit and a 5' 6" Eye Level :

a) A point 6' from near corner and 12' high on front face of double cube.

b) A point 12" behind, on the square plan, of point a.

c) A point 4' in front of the face 17' from near corner, 3' high.

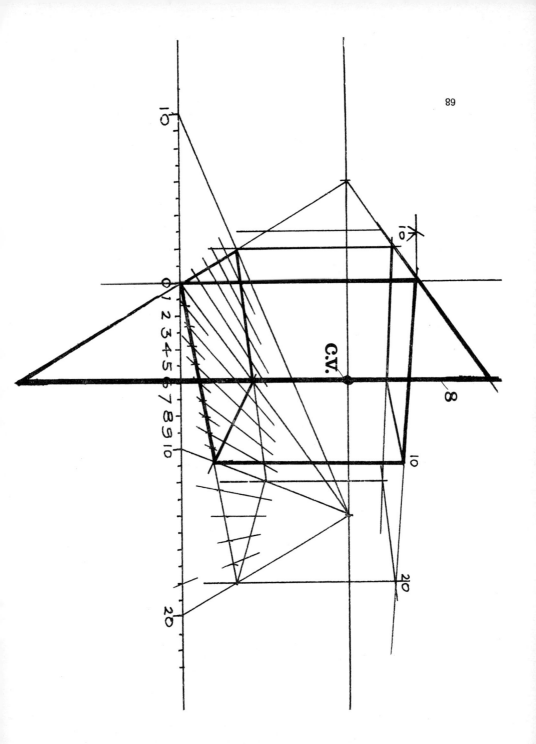

10

10

0 1 2 3 4 5 6 7 8 9 10

C.V.

8

10

20

20

13.0/ Further development of grid

13.1/ Familiarity with the oblique perspective construction **a–z** above and of principles involved will reveal alternative methods of setting-up procedure. For rapid and freehand sketch perspectives the following notes show simple developments of the basic grid.

13.2/ Vertical **8** is on the Central line of Vision. Where it crosses the Eye Level is the Centre of Vision. It defines the rear corner of the front cube ; divides the front square in half ; defines the full square forward plane with the left hand side of the nearest cube (i.e. below the Base Line).

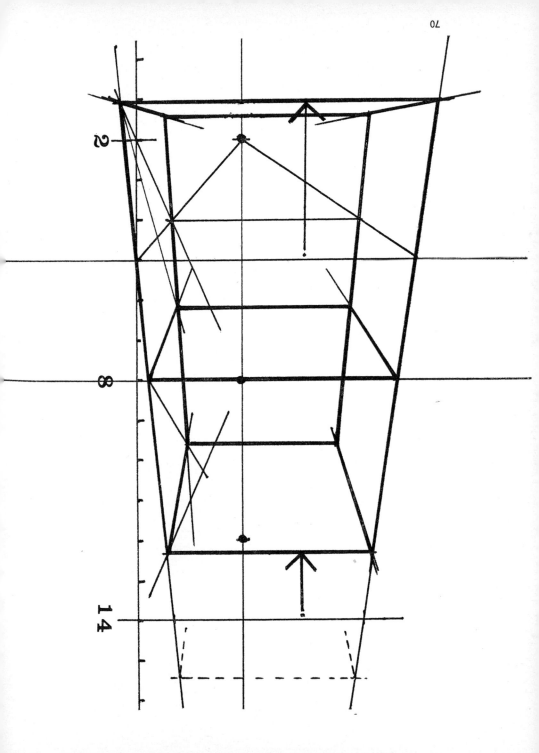

13.3/ Lines drawn from the Centre of Vision through points **2**, **8** and **14** on Base Line cube the front plane of the double cube at the half squares. From these points another double cube grid may be constructed—removed half square to the left (using 45° diagonals to Viewpoint 12). This allows one more cube on the right, i. e. 3 in a row to occur within the Cone of Vision. This gives the maximum width along the face of the grid that can be normally set up in rapid oblique method (see 13.6.3).

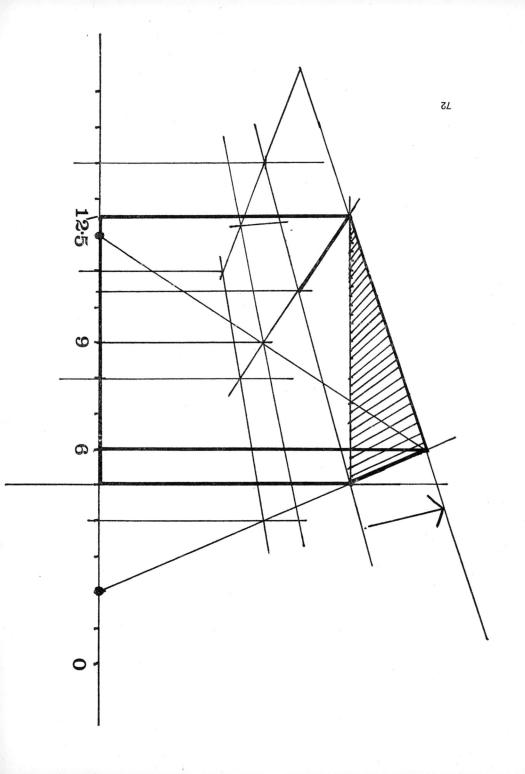

13.4/ Vertical **6** defines the half square *forward* in plane with the side of front cube (in front of Base Line). Vertical **9** halves the centre square that divides the double cube. The top and bottom of these verticals may be joined by the 45° diagonal to the Vanishing Point **12**. Vertical **12½** gives the half square forward in plane with the square that divides cubes. It occurs on the Picture Plane and scales the same as at Vertical **5**. From these points another cube grid, remove half a square forward, nearer the Observer, may be constructed. In this diagram, as a further demonstration of points in the notes : the grid has been mirrored, the Eye Level is at zero height, and the shaded area is both forward of the Picture Plane and (independently) outside the Cone of Vision.

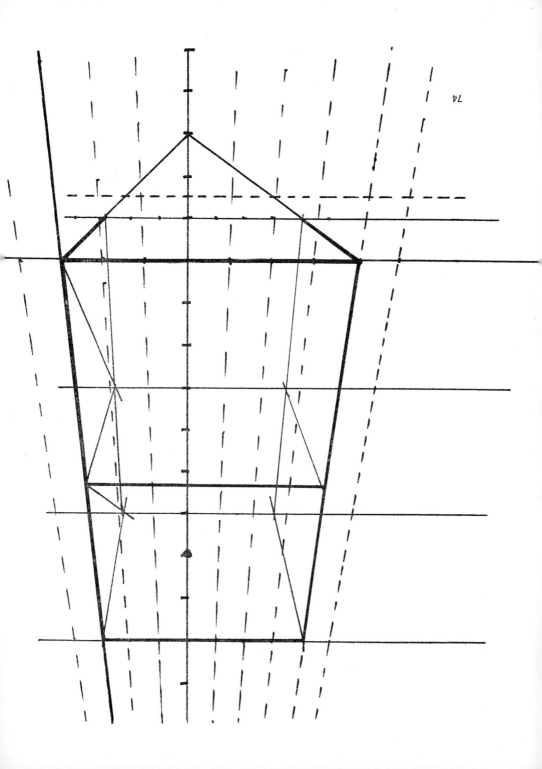

13.5/ The rapid method of this book provides an accurate means for a set up perspective but the first intention is that of speed, especially for the draughtsman who needs a basis for freehand perspectives to analyse and present his proposals. For this purpose the basic grid can be drawn up quickly for any size scale and Eye Level.

For simple subjects useful guidelines can be quickly set up showing the major verticals and a regular grid of lines converging between verticals **5** and **14**. For a series of drawings, say for comparison purposes, a standard diagram for a fixed size, scale and Eye Level should be made (see page 82).

13.6/ For the **a** to **z** method and the freehand developments the standard draughtsman scales, by chance, give the 1 : 3 ratio of the heights measured at verticals **5** and **14**, and can be employed usefully on a half-imperial board (A2 international size).

i) Having determined the scale to be represented (as below), heights can be measured directly:

Vertical **5**   using $1\frac{1}{2}''$ to 1' scale   i. e. FS cn Picture Plane
Vertical **4 & 14**   using $1''$ to 1' scale   i. e. FS cn Picture Plane
Vertical **3$\frac{1}{2}$ & 11**   using $\frac{3}{4}''$ to 1' scale   i. e. $\frac{1}{2}$ FS 2 on Picture Plane

Lines joining a height measured in this way on two verticals, establishes the perspective automatically.

ii) As a rule of thumb, taking a nominal 5' 0" Eye Level, the maximum height at the Picture Plane may be selected for each subject, as follows:

with a scale $1\frac{1}{2}''$ = 1' to give 5' + 7' = 12'
$1\frac{1}{2}''$ = 2' to give 5' + 14' = 19' (i. e. using $\frac{3}{4}''$ = 1' scale)
$1\frac{1}{2}''$ = 4' to give 5' + 28' = 33' (i. e. using $\frac{3}{8}''$ = 1' scale) etc.

iii) Associated lengths along the face of the double cube grid that are contained within the Cone of Vision are:

$1\frac{1}{2}''$ = 1' — 21'
$1\frac{1}{2}''$ = 2' — 42'
$1\frac{1}{2}''$ = 4' — 84' (see 12.4 and 13.3)

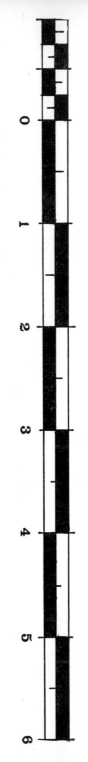

iv) With these vertical scales the Depth Scale (alternative II) is converted to 5/7th ratio. This scale is the correct Full Size *Depth Scale* for $1\frac{1}{2}''$ vertical units.

v) Similarly, with the $1\frac{1}{2}''$ units in the decimal (alternative I) method the Height Scale is converted to 7/5th ratio. This *decimal* scale is the correct Full Size *Height Scale* for $1\frac{1}{2}''$ Base line units.

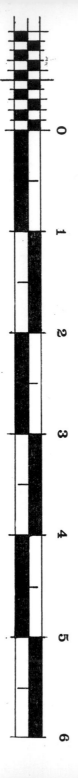

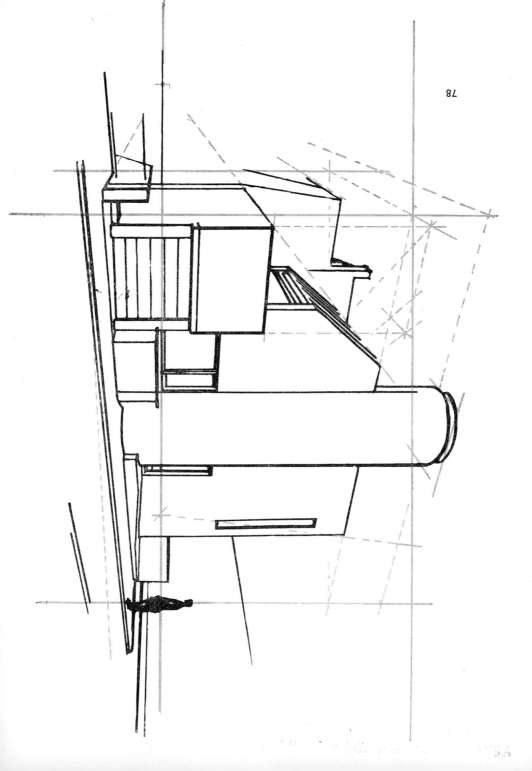

EXAMPLE OF OBLIQUE PERSPECTIVE.

This illustration shows all the construction necessary to produce this exterior perspective.

House in Kensington Place by Tom Kay, ARIBA